ZAGATSURVEY®

25TH ANNIVERSARY

2005

CALIFORNIA WINE COUNTRY RESTAURANTS

Local Editor: Meesha Halm

Local Coordinator: Maura Sell

Editor: Troy Segal

Published and distributed by
ZAGAT SURVEY, LLC
4 Columbus Circle
New York, New York 10019
Tel: 212 977 6000
E-mail: californiawine@zagat.com
Web site: www.zagat.com

Acknowledgments

We thank Antonia Allegra, Alissa Bushnell, Erica Curtis, Heidi Cusick, Jon, Olive and Jude Fox, Vincent, Conor and Liam Logan, Leroy Meshel, Steven Shukow, Jeffrey Tappan and Willow Waldeck, as well as the following members of our staff: Reni Chin, Larry Cohn, Anuradha Duggal, Schuyler Frazier, Jeff Freier, Shelley Gallagher, Katherine Harris, Natalie Lebert, Mike Liao, Dave Makulec, Emily Parsons, Robert Poole, Rob Seixas, Kelly Sinanis, Yoji Yamaguchi and Sharon Yates.

What's New

Like a fine bottle of Cabernet, California's wine-country restaurants just keep getting better with age. And as their strong presence on the Tops lists of our *2005 San Francisco Restaurant Survey* – the source for this pocket guide – suggests, their renown spreads across the Bay Area, with many becoming destinations in their own right.

Sonoma Thinks Small: Most of the noteworthy newcomers have opened in this viticultural valley of late. Entrants such as Willi's Seafood in Healdsburg and Harmony Club in the town of Sonoma are proving that the small-plates concept, so popular in SF, plays perfectly in the land of the *petit* Syrah, too – so many dishes, so many opportunities for wine-pairing.

Napa's Gourmet Ghetto: In fact, one such food-and-vino showcase, Wine Garden Food and Wine Bar, was slated at press time to open in Yountville. This town remains the wine country's culinary epicenter, and this year, some of its biggest guns were making news. After a five-month hiatus, Thomas Keller reopened his freshened French Laundry, and Philippe Jeanty unveiled the Provençal Père Jeanty, just a stone's throw from his original eponymous eatery. Nearby, in Downtown Napa, the Food Network's Pilar Sanchez launched Pilar, whose Cal menu will feature the valley's bounty, while the folks behind the popular Wappo Bar Bistro opened a modest sibling, Wappo Taco.

Mendocino Rising: Noyo Harbor, a picturesque fishing town in Fort Bragg, is shaping up to be the wine country's equivalent of Off-Broadway, a low-rent breeding ground for hopefuls destined for the big time. The funky pier-side Sharon's By the Sea, run by Sharon Morgan, opened an offshoot in the Hill House Inn. Conversely, chef Colleen Murphy traded in her tony Mendocino Hotel address for her own low-key riverside digs, Chapter and Moon, which showcases her inventive American cuisine.

September 28, 2004   Meesha Halm

Top 50 Food

Except where indicated by a ∇, the list excludes places with low voting. An asterisk indicates a tie.

28 French Laundry
27 Farmhouse Inn∇
Café La Haye
La Toque
26 Rest. at Stevenswood
Terra
Bistro Jeanty
Auberge du Soleil
25 Cole's Chop Hse.
Madrona Manor
Martini Hse.
Willi's Seafood
Hana Japanese
24 Tra Vigne
Bistro Don Giov.
Mustards Grill
Cafe Beaujolais
Willi's Wine Bar
Foothill Cafe
Syrah
Domaine Chandon
Downtown Bakery
Bouchon
zazu
John Ash & Co.

Gordon's
Santi
LaSalette
23 Ravenous
Kenwood
Cafe Lolo
MacCallum Hse.
Albion River Inn
Little River Inn
Dry Creek Kit.
Villa Corona
Della Santina's
Julia's Kitchen
Zuzu
Ledford Hse.
Wappo Bar
Wine Spectator
22 Cindy's Backstreet
Taylor's Automatic*
All Season's Cafe
Celadon
Manzanita
Meadowood Grill
Angèle
girl & the fig

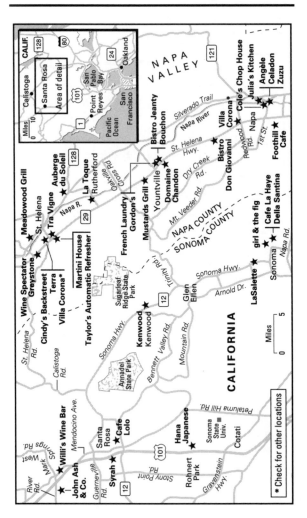

Map of Napa Valley and Sonoma County restaurant locations:

- Cole's Chop House
- Julia's Kitchen
- Angèle
- Celadon
- Zuzu
- Villa Corona
- Bistro Jeanty
- Bouchon
- Bistro Don Giovanni
- Foothill Cafe
- Meadowood Grill
- Tra Vigne
- Auberge du Soleil
- La Toque
- Rutherford
- Domaine Chandon
- French Laundry
- Gordon's
- Mustards Grill
- Yountville
- Cafe La Haye
- Della Santina
- girl & the fig
- Wine Spectator Greystone
- Terra
- Cindy's Backstreet
- Villa Corona*
- Martini House
- Taylor's Automatic Refresher
- LaSalette
- Sonoma
- Kenwood
- Will's Wine Bar
- Cafe Lolo
- Hana Japanese
- John Ash & Co.
- Syrah

NAPA VALLEY
NAPA COUNTY
SONOMA COUNTY
CALIFORNIA

CALIF. · Calistoga · Santa Rosa · Area of detail · Oakland · San Pablo Bay · Point Reyes · San Francisco · Pacific Ocean

Miles 0 10

Silverado Trail
Napa River
St. Helena Hwy.
Dry Creek Rd.
Redwood Rd.
1st St.
Mt. Veeder Rd.
Napa R.
Oakville Cross Rd.
Trinity Rd.
Sonoma Hwy.
Arnold Dr.
Napa Rd.
St. Helena Rd.
Calistoga Rd.
Sugarloaf Ridge State Park
Annadel State Park
Bennett Valley Rd.
Mountain Rd.
Glen Ellen
Kenwood
Sonoma
Sonoma State Univ.
Cotati
Rohnert Park
Santa Rosa
Guerneville Rd.
Mendocino Ave.
Mark West Springs Rd.
River Rd.
Stony Point Rd.
Gravenstein Hwy.
Petaluma Hill Rd.

Miles 0 5

* Check for other locations

Top Food

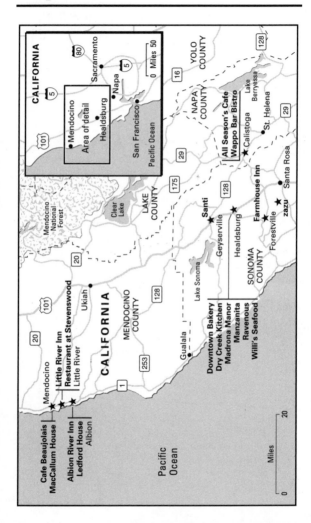

subscribe to zagat.com

Ratings & Symbols

Name, Address, Phone Number & Web Site

Hours & Credit Cards

Zagat Ratings

F	D	S	C
▽ 23	9	13	$15

Tim & Nina's ◑ 🎦 ⊅

9999 Lincoln Ave. (Washington St.), Calistoga, 707-555-1234; www.zagat.com

☑ Open "more or less when T & N sober up", this Calistoga cafe–cum–wine bar offers "casual", "real Cal cuisine" – i.e. "it's picked outside the back door", and the wine comes straight "out of their bathtub"; it all tastes "surprisingly good" and is (literally) "dirt cheap" – that is, if you can ever get attention from one of the "tippling waiters."

Review, with surveyors' comments in quotes

Restaurants with Top Ratings or Importance are printed in CAPITAL LETTERS.

Before reviews a symbol indicates whether responses were uniform ■ or mixed ☑.

Hours: ◑ serves after 11 PM
🎦 closed on Sunday

Credit Cards: ⊅ no credit cards accepted

Ratings: Food, Decor and Service are rated on a scale of **0** to **30**. The Cost (C) column reflects our surveyors' estimate of the price of dinner including one drink and tip.

F	Food	D	Decor	S	Service	C	Cost
23		9		13		$15	

0–9 poor to fair	**20–25** very good to excellent
10–15 fair to good	**26–30** extraordinary to perfection
16–19 good to very good	▽ low response/less reliable

For places listed without ratings, such as a newcomer or write-in, the price range is indicated as follows:

I	$25 and below	**E**	$41 to $65
M	$26 to $40	**VE**	$66 or more

ALBION RIVER INN　　23 ｜ 22 ｜ 23 ｜ $47

3790 North Hwy. 1 (Albion Little River Rd.), Albion, 707-937-1919;
www.albionriverinn.com

■ "For a quick getaway", head to this "dreamy, romantic spot perched atop a cliff overlooking the ocean" in Albion where you can "watch a pod of whales play" and the "sunset during dinner"; while the "excellent" Cal coastal cuisine "rarely breaks new ground (or should that be water?)", the wine list is "mind-boggling" and the service "convivial"; and should you consume a little too much "rare scotch" from their "spectacular collection", you can always stay the night.

Alexander Valley Grille　　21 ｜ 26 ｜ 20 ｜ $38

(fka Chateau Souverain Café at the Winery)
400 Souverain Rd. (Hwy. 101, Independence Ln. exit), Geyserville,
707-433-3141; www.chateausouverain.com

■ With "incredible views" "overlooking the vineyards" and "proprietary" "vino suggestions with each entrée", this Geyserville winery/eatery offers "the consummate wine-country experience" ("it's where we take guests when we want to make them envious of where we live"); while the "fine Cal-French cuisine" and "attentive service" "don't match the setting", "drunk or sober", "you can't beat it in the summer" on the "beautiful outdoor patio" or "in the cold of winter when the fireplaces are aglow."

Alexis Baking Company　　22 ｜ 11 ｜ 14 ｜ $16

(aka ABC)
1517 Third St. (School St.), Napa, 707-258-1827;
www.alexisbakingcompany.com

◪ It "wouldn't be Saturday without" a visit to this Downtown Napa "institution" crammed with bakery devotees who find it "worth the wait in line" for "excellent coffee drinks", "creative breakfast offerings" ("of note: the huevos rancheros"), "divine cakes" and "down-home" New American lunches; however, don't expect much from the "disinterested" staff.

ALL SEASON'S CAFE & WINE SHOP

22 | 16 | 20 | $38

1400 Lincoln Ave. (Washington St.), Calistoga, 707-942-9111; www.allseasonsnapavalley.com

■ Offering "no-nonsense" "seasonal" Californian–New French fare "paired with the fine wines" found in "the shop next door" (which they serve *sans* markup), this "totally unpretentious" Calistoga eatery is where "all the local vintners" and their families dine; while the "fantastic food" and "knowledgeable staff" are certainly "worthy of celebratory evenings", the "casual" "converted-storefront" ambiance may seem more appropriate for lunch after winery-hopping.

ANGÈLE

22 | 22 | 21 | $41

540 Main St. (3rd St.), Napa, 707-252-8115; www.angele.us

◪ Although "the tourists haven't found their way" into this "simpatico bistro" – yet – locals insist it's "one of the best" in "Napa's emerging restaurant scene", where "comfortable" "country-style French" food, an "adorable bar", "attentive service" and "romantic" "riverside dining" "equal a winning combination"; however, most prefer the "lovely outdoor patio" over the somewhat "spartan", "wood-beamed" interior.

Applewood Inn & Restaurant

▽ 24 | 20 | 21 | $46

13555 Hwy. 116 (River Rd.), Guerneville, 707-869-9093; www.applewoodinn.com

■ Nestled in a "beautiful inn near the Russian River", this "quiet" "romantic" is "about as cozy as you'll find with two fireplaces" and "nice forest views", but even more dazzling is what's happening at the table; the "great new chef (ex Zazu) is really strutting her stuff" whipping up "excellent" locally driven Cal cuisine, while "helpful, informative waiters" are on hand to pair something from their "great wine list"; P.S. "Sunday-Monday Italian nights are screaming bargains."

AUBERGE DU SOLEIL   26 | 27 | 25 | $69

Auberge du Soleil, 180 Rutherford Hill Rd. (Silverado Trail), Rutherford, 707-967-3111; www.aubergedusoleil.com

■ "Few experiences are more romantic" than this "exclusive Rutherford resort" where you "overlook a picture-postcard view" while sampling something off the "unbelievable" wine list and being "pampered by the staff"; while "even a frozen dinner would taste great" here, the "luscious" French-Med prix fixe is "so worth the price tag" – though locals "suggest stopping for lunch" for "better vistas at half the price"; N.B. the arrival of chef Joseph Humphrey (ex Fifth Floor) postdates the Food score.

BayLeaf Restaurant   ▽ 19 | 22 | 19 | $44

2025 Monticello Rd. (Vichy St.), Napa, 707-257-9720; www.bayleafnapa.com

☑ The jury is still out on this "romantic" Napa newcomer, an unapologetically "old-fashioned" kind of place, with "a tuxedoed host", valet parking and American "food from an another era" (think beef Wellington); its "fan club" appreciates the "elegant" warren of rooms, but modernists moan this "pretentious" place "doesn't work in the Valley."

Belle Arti   ▽ 19 | 19 | 18 | $31

1040 Main St. (bet. 1st & Pearl Sts.), Napa, 707-255-0720; www.bellearti-napa.com

☑ This "*belissimo*" bistro boasts a "lovely setting" "next to the river in Downtown Napa" and "straightforward" Sicilian *cucina* that's "a welcome change from standard Italian"; but while "good prices and friendly service" have made it into a "locals' spot", tourists counter "competition is too tough" for an "uneven", "unmemorable" experience.

BISTRO DON GIOVANNI   24 | 22 | 22 | $42

4110 Howard Ln. (bet. Oak Knoll & Salvador Aves.), Napa, 707-224-3300; www.bistrodongiovanni.com

■ It's "no wonder the parking lot's always full" at this "consummate" "wine-country bistro" "in the heart of

Napa"; the "hearty food" tastes "as if California mated with Tuscany", "the servers are in overdrive" and the "stylish" "boisterous" room is "always packed" with an "exuberant" mix of tourists, vintners and locals; "you'd be hard-pressed to find a better scene" partisans pronounce, particularly "sitting on the patio looking out over the vineyards."

BISTRO JEANTY 26 | 21 | 23 | $45

6510 Washington St. (Mulberry St.), Yountville, 707-944-0103; www.bistrojeanty.com

■ Featuring "scrumptious", "soul-satisfying" "classic French bistro cuisine", "quaint" "farmhouse decor" and "*très bien*" service, Philippe Jeanty's "wine-country 'in'-spot" (and "offal lover's paradise") "succeeds in making you feel" like "you could be in Paris" "right here in Yountville"; *oui*, it's "noisy and cramped", but in the chef-owner's "expanding culinary empire, it remains the stalwart" and "well worth" "*le détour*"; P.S. spontaneous types can "just sit at the bar" or the "communal table for drop-ins."

Bistro Ralph ⌧ 22 | 17 | 20 | $39

109 Plaza St. (Healdsburg Ave.), Healdsburg, 707-433-1380

■ Despite a myriad of newcomers to Healdsburg, Ralph Tingle's boisterous, busy little bistro, located just off the "Rockwell-esque town square", remains a "longtime favorite" among acolytes who relish the "excellent New American" menu made with "fresh Sonoma Valley products" and a varietal "list heavily weighted to local entries"; and while the "friendly" servers "know more about wine than a sommelier", they also proffer a martini "big enough to swim in."

Bistrot La Poste ∇ 25 | 15 | 20 | $41

599 Broadway Ave. (Patton St.), Sonoma, 707-939-3663; www.bistrotlaposte.com

☑ "Be prepared to have a good time" and make "new *amis*" at this "cheerful", "casual" "postage-stamp–size

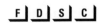
bistro" in Sonoma, "since it's like you're all sitting around having dinner together"; while the "cramped space" "could be a little difficult" for claustrophobics, it helps that the textbook French food and wine are "wonderful" and the service "boisterous and sincere."

Boonville Hotel ▽ 22 | 21 | 19 | $40
Boonville Hotel, 14050 Hwy. 128 (Lambert Ln.), Boonville, 707-895-2210; www.boonvillehotel.com
■ In the midst of "the Anderson Valley viticultural region", this "nicely restored old hotel" is a "great place to stop on your way to or from Mendocino", offering a daily changing selection of "simple" but "well-executed" Cal–New American eats and "friendly service" in the "lovely" Shaker-style dining room and bar; however, despite it being "way off the beaten path", expect interstate prices.

BOUCHON ◗ 24 | 22 | 21 | $46
6534 Washington St. (Yount St.), Yountville, 707-944-8037; www.frenchlaundry.com
◪ "French bistro fare as good as any in Paris" and "a happening late-night scene" make this Thomas Keller creation a "welcome consolation" "to those who can't get in, or just refuse to pay" for his "more famous" Yountville place; yes, "tables are tight" (lots of "patron interaction") and the "room's loud, but it's still a great wine-country experience", especially if you sit at the "awesome" zinc bar with chefs and other "interesting folks from town and beyond"; P.S. they've got a "bakery next door."

Brannan's Grill 20 | 21 | 20 | $37
1374 Lincoln Ave. (Washington St.), Calistoga, 707-942-2233; www.brannansgrill.com
◪ Departing from the "quintessential charm of Calistoga", this "lively" lair evokes an "East Coast feel" with "heavy wood", "intimate lighting and cozy booths"; it's the go-to place when you are hankering for some "hearty" New American fare and a "wonderful wine selection" "without

the Napa Valley prices"; but critics carp it "looks better than it tastes" – or treats guests ("the servers may as well be in Vallejo").

Brasserie de la Mer ▽ 19 16 17 $40

Vineyard Creek Hotel, 170 Railroad St. (W. 3rd St.), Santa Rosa, 707-636-7388

◪ "A fine selection" of seafood, a good value of an "early-bird prix fixe" and a "romantic, cozy fireplace bar" ("tip: ask to be seated" there) all make this Santa Rosa French bistro "better than the usual convention-center restaurant"; however, the "Denny's-like" "look detracts from the dining experience", as does an unseasoned staff that "needs some love."

Brix 21 22 20 $44

7377 St. Helena Hwy./Hwy. 29 (Washington St.), Yountville, 707-944-2749; www.brix.com

■ Although it's "not as famous as some", this "casual" Yountviller "holds its own amid tough wine-country competition" with its "glamorous" setting featuring "unobstructed views of the hills, vineyards and gardens" – the latter providing produce for the "creative" Cal cuisine; all allow the "Sunday brunch is a dream-come-true for any local or tourist", but views diverge on the adjacent wine/gift shop ("commercial" vs. "nice").

CAFE BEAUJOLAIS 24 20 21 $48

961 Ukiah St. (School St.), Mendocino, 707-937-5614; www.cafebeaujolais.com

■ "Still one of the best on the North Coast", this "charming bungalow" with lovely gardens and rustic bakery out back is always "buzzing" with the "easygoing Mendo crowd" and savvy tourists who "drive three hours from SF" just to savor the "wonderful breads" and Cal-French menu that's "simplicity rediscovered"; some still pine for "the old days" under original owner Margaret Fox, but most find the "relaxed feel" and "attentive" staff "live on."

Cafe Citti
20 | 11 | 16 | $21

9049 Sonoma Hwy./Hwy. 12 (Shaw Ave.), Kenwood, 707-833-2690
■ "A locals' favorite", this "informal" family-friendly "roadhouse" serving "awesome rotisserie chicken" and "wonderful" "Northern Italian trattoria food" at "budget-conscious" prices is a "good place to fill up" en route to or from "your favorite winery" in Kenwood; just "forget the atmosphere" (or lack thereof) and concept of service (as you "order from a counter").

CAFÉ LA HAYE
27 | 20 | 25 | $40

140 E. Napa St. (bet. 1st & 2nd Sts.), Sonoma, 707-935-5994;
www.cafelahaye.com
■ "It's unbelievable what chef John McReynolds creates in his tiny kitchen" at this "always fun" Cal–New American that he co-owns with Saul Gropman, who oversees the "compact", "art"-oriented room and "lovely" service; many feel it's "one of the best in Sonoma", as well as a "value", because the food based on "fresh items from local markets and farms" is "outstanding" and the wine list "worthy" of the locale.

CAFE LOLO ⌧
23 | 17 | 21 | $40

620 Fifth St. (Santa Rosa Ave.), Santa Rosa, 707-576-7822;
www.cafelolo.com
■ "A real Santa Rosa favorite", this "small" New American is "a standby" for locals thanks to consistently "solid" fare, "great wine" and "friendly" service; but some sense "it's getting tired" and "needs to get its winning energy back"; in particular, a "remodeling" would tame the "noise level."

Calistoga Inn
Restaurant & Brewery
19 | 18 | 18 | $30

Calistoga Inn, 1250 Lincoln Ave. (Cedar St.), Calistoga,
707-942-4101; www.calistogainn.com
■ "Hip restaurants have come and gone", but this "folksy" Calistoga brewpub has been a steadfast "fixture", supplying "straightforward", if "inconsistent", Cal fare and "crafty"

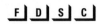
"homemade beers"; but everyone agrees "the best thing" about the joint is not the "dark, uninviting dining room" but the "creek-side" patio that's "sublime on summer evenings."

Carneros
∇ 23 | 19 | 20 | $43

The Lodge at Sonoma, 1325 Broadway (Leveroni Rd.), Sonoma, 707-931-2042; www.thelodgeatsonoma.com

☑ Set in a Sonoma hotel, this Californian offers a "splurge night out in the wine country" with a menu that makes "excellent use of the area's bounty" and plenty of vintages from the region; not everyone warms to the "somewhat corporate setting", and some add that while it's a "solid" choice, "there are better in the area"; N.B. a recent chef change may outdate the Food score.

CELADON
22 | 20 | 22 | $40

Napa Mills, 500 Main St. (5th St.), Napa, 707-254-9690

■ Greg Cole's "hidden treasure" in the Napa Mills complex serves New American fare that "we're all familiar with" but adds "special touches and creative pairings", plus an "interesting wine list", "to keep it fresh and worth repeat business"; service is "attentive but not obtrusive" and if the decor leaves some "feeling cold", the patio with an "outdoor fireplace is incredibly romantic."

Cena Luna ☒
– | – | – | M

241 Healdsburg Ave. (Matheson St.), Healdsburg, 707-433-6000; www.cenaluna.com

This 68-seat newcomer in Healdsburg is an exercise in simplicity, thanks to a weekly changing menu that offers a dozen or so regional Italian dishes (half of which feature housemade pasta) and a wine list heavy on local Sonoma picks; the dining room is old-world chic with handsome dark-cherry-wood wainscoting and a myriad of mirrors.

Chapter and Moon
∇ 18 | 15 | 15 | $25

32150 N. Harbor Dr. (Shoreline Hwy.), Fort Bragg, 707-962-1643

☑ Although "hidden behind a trailer park", this newish "sweet spot on Noyo Harbor" in Fort Bragg has "nice water views" and "former Mendocino Hotel chef Colleen Murphy at the helm", cooking American "comfort food dressed up for a formal outing"; critics note the menu's "a little ambitious and should be simplified", but concede it's "needed" in these parts, especially since "you can't beat the prices."

Charcuterie   21 | 16 | 19 | $31 |
335 Healdsburg Ave. (Plaza St.), Healdsburg, 707-431-7213
■ The "decor is all pigs – and you'll feel like one after you leave" this "quaint" corner offering "locals and tourists alike" a "limited" but "well-executed" menu of French "comfort food" classics (think duck confit, salade niçoise) and "a simple wine list to match"; throw in a "friendly staff", and it all seems reminiscent of a "Paris bistro", even though it's smack dab "in the heart of Healdsburg."

Chez Felice   – | – | – | M |
716 McClelland Dr. (Windsor Town Green), Windsor, 707-836-9922
Run by the owners of nearby Château Felice Winery, this casual new bistro/tasting bar/retail shop sits on the Windsor Town Green; chef Laurie Souza (who's cooked at sundry wineries, most recently Kenwood) prepares a Med-inspired menu that includes a 'Flights of Fancy' section, pairing small plates with wines, from Felice's own vintages to a collection of older French and California 'library' bottles.

CINDY'S BACKSTREET KITCHEN   22 | 19 | 19 | $35 |
1327 Railroad Ave. (bet. Adams & Hunt Sts.), St. Helena, 707-963-1200
■ "Similar Cal–New American comfort food" given "the Napa touch" to chef-owner "Cindy Pawlcyn's sister restaurant" prompts patrons to dub her "re-created" "St. Helena hot spot" "Mustards Grill North" – minus the "tourist glitz"; there's "good cheer all around" the "quaint" digs – "even the waiters seem to be having fun" – especially if you join the "local wine crowd" "out on the garden patio."

COLE'S CHOP HOUSE   25 | 23 | 23 | $52

1122 Main St. (bet. 1st & Pearl Sts.), Napa, 707-224-6328
■ When they need "to offset all that fancy wine-country" cuisine, carnivores corral at this "*Gunsmoke*"-esque site (think "wooden bar and rock walls"); though it specializes in "steaks the size of an Oldsmobile", it also appeals to non-meatheads with "some of the best seafood around"; beefy prices save it "for expense accounts and power dinners with winemakers", but with "friendly servers" pouring "wicked martinis" and "classic Napa Cabernets", "why clog the arteries anywhere else?"

Cucina Paradiso   ▽ 22 | 15 | 23 | $30

Golden Eagle Shopping Ctr., 56 E. Washington St. (Petaluma Blvd.), Petaluma, 707-782-1130
■ Don't let the "strip-mall storefront" fool you – this "marvelous little Southern Italian" is "one of the better spots in Petaluma" with "consistently excellent" *cucina*, "accommodating service" and such niceties as "white tablecloths, napkins and fresh flowers"; there's even a seasonal patio ("next to the parking lot", granted), which "allows you to bring your dog", if you're so inclined.

DELLA SANTINA'S   23 | 19 | 21 | $34

133 E. Napa St. (1st St. E.), Sonoma, 707-935-0576;
www.dellasantinas.com
■ "For a *bella notte*", locals head to this "old-world" trattoria just "off Sonoma Square", where the Tuscan fare, including "great items from the rotisserie", and a "charming" Decor score–boosting garden patio transport you to "Italy without the eight-hour flight"; "service can be slow" but it's nothing the ever-present "endearing owner" can't fix.

Deuce   ▽ 20 | 20 | 22 | $36

691 Broadway (Andrieux St.), Sonoma, 707-933-3823;
www.dine-at-deuce.com
☑ Surveyors have dueling views about this Sonoma New American, set in a converted Victorian farmhouse;

fanciers feel the "new chef is hitting his stride" and appreciate the "truly great" locally leaning wine list, "lovely leafy patio" and "friendly staff"; foes fret "for the price, we expected a little better" than food, decor and service "without much flair."

DOMAINE CHANDON   24 25 24 $61
1 California Dr. (Hwy. 29), Yountville, 707-944-2892; www.chandon.com

■ If "sparkling wine with each course" is your "idea of heaven", then "finish off a tour of the champagne facility" with a tasting menu at this "beautiful indoor/outdoor" winery restaurant set on "romantic" "sylvan" grounds; gourmets grin that new chef Ron Boyd's "exquisite" Californian menu has "put this back on the Yountville food map", the service remains "elegance defined" and a recent remodel should bring some extra fizz to the 25-year-old dining room; it's "expensive", but an "epicurean delight."

DOWNTOWN BAKERY & CREAMERY ☞   24 11 15 $11
308A Center St. (Matheson St.), Healdsburg, 707-431-2719; www.downtownbakery.net

☑ "Ok, so it's not a restaurant per se" but this "fantastic" Healdsburg bakery does serve "spectacular" sandwiches and "pastry, ice cream and coffee – what more do you need?"; "service can be almost rude, but then you don't have to stay long", just seize your share of the "irresistible" treats and join the "locals and their dogs" who "hang out on two benches outside" or in the square.

DRY CREEK KITCHEN   23 23 19 $54
Hotel Healdsburg, 317 Healdsburg Ave. (Matheson St.), Healdsburg, 707-431-0330; www.hotelhealdsburg.com

☑ There's "big-city dining" in them Maycamas hills – specifically, at Charlie Palmer's "ultramodern" venture "adjacent to the Euro-chic Hotel Healdsburg" that's "raised the bar" for the region with its "aesthetically prepared"

New American cuisine complemented by an "all-Sonoma (and all good) wine list" (and "no corkage fee" if you bring your own); however, compliments dry up when it comes to the service, which many moan is quite "inconsistent" – and "at NYC prices", it shouldn't be.

Duck Club, The 20 | 21 | 20 | $42 |

Bodega Bay Lodge & Spa, 103 Coast Hwy. 1 (Doran Park Rd.), Bodega, 707-875-3525; www.bodegabaylodge.com

■ A "quiet, clubby atmosphere" prevails at this "special-occasion" spot, catering to a mix of "venture capitalists", "blue hairs" and students with "parents in town"; it's "as good as it gets" for suburban hotel dining, with "well-done", "if not spectacular" New American dinners (though the signature dish "puts all other ducks to shame"), and a "beautiful view of Bodega Bay."

FARMHOUSE INN & RESTAURANT, THE ∇ 27 | 26 | 26 | $53 |

Farmhouse Inn, 7871 River Rd. (Wohler Rd.), Forestville, 707-887-3300; www.farmhouseinn.com

■ "One of the best-kept secrets in the wine country... until now", this "splurge-worthy" "brother-and-sister–run" Forestville getaway embodies "what Sonoma is all about"; guests swoon over a "daily changing" Cal menu based on "whatever is fresh and in season" and the "impeccable" locally leaning wine list, "not to mention the cheese cart and the gracious service"; the overall effect is "like dining in someone's fancy dining room", which, in a way, it is.

fig cafe & winebar ∇ 22 | 19 | 23 | $38 |
(fka the girl & the gaucho)

13690 Arnold Dr. (Warm Springs Rd.), Glen Ellen, 707-938-2130; www.thefigcafe.com

■ Owner Sondra Bernstein has transformed her Latin-leaning Glen Ellen eatery into a "more casual" "country cousin" of her the girl & the fig and the result is a place now "packed on weekends"; fans will recognize the same "laid-back, friendly" staff serving "reasonably priced" Provençal-inspired comfort dishes, but it's the wine that's "the real standout here."

FOOTHILL CAFE   24 14 21 $35
J&P Shopping Ctr., 2766 Old Sonoma Rd. (Foothill Blvd.), Napa, 707-252-6178
◪ A "crummy strip-mall setting" hides one of "Napa's best kept secrets" – this "reasonably priced" "source for ribs" and other "well-prepared" all-American barbecue-type eats that's "made a name for itself in the Valley"; those who "schlep" out of their way to find it are sometimes disappointed by "overcrowded" conditions and "significant waits", but others affirm it's "a must every summer."

FRENCH LAUNDRY   28 26 27 $135
6640 Washington St. (Creek St.), Yountville, 707-944-2380; www.frenchlaundry.com
■ Enthusiasts are "excited about returning" to Thomas Keller's reopened Yountville institution; the "Herculean effort" "to get a reservation could lead to disappointment" but they "wow you", from the "impeccably served" French–New American menus, "a whirlwind" of tiny tastes and big sensations, to the "gorgeous gardens" or "understated" interior; a few snap it's "stuffy", literally and figuratively, but to most, "no prose can do justice" to this "once-in-a-lifetime experience (twice on someone else's dime)."

Fumé Bistro & Bar   ▽ 21 18 21 $33
4050 Byway St. E. (Wine Country Ave.), Napa, 707-257-1999; www.fumebistro.com
■ Although "it almost fades into the background with all the famous restaurants around", this Napa New American bistro is too "good to be forgotten" says a "mostly local" clientele that includes "winemakers sneaking a quick lunch away from the crowds" and others who likewise appreciate the "friendly" service, "comfortable, casual" atmosphere and outdoor seating.

Gary Chu's   21 | 18 | 20 | $30 |

611 Fifth St. (bet. D & Mendocino Sts.), Santa Rosa, 707-526-5840;
www.garychus.com

■ "The Chu empire seems to be expanding" in other Asian territories, but "what brings back the crowds" to his eponymous flagship in Downtown Santa Rosa are his "upscale", and some would say "Westernized", renditions of Chinese staples served in a "classier" atmosphere than others of its ilk ("you won't see ducks in the window" here); N.B. a work-in-progress remodel may outdate the Decor score.

General's Daughter, The   19 | 23 | 21 | $39 |

400 W. Spain St. (bet. 4th & 5th Sts.), Sonoma, 707-938-4004;
www.thegeneralsdaughter.com

☑ You can't touch the "attractive setting" and sense of history of this "country cute" Californian set in an 1864 house "built by General Vallejo for his daughter" and boasting "lovely" gardens and a patio that's "perfect" for "drinking in the beauty of Sonoma"; while it's a hit "with the tourists", the food quality is "uneven" and the room "noisy", leading some to demote it to "The Sergeant's Daughter."

Geyser Smokehouse   ▽ 15 | 14 | 16 | $22 |

21021 Geyserville Ave. (Hwy. 128), Geyserville, 707-857-4600;
www.geysersmokehouse.com

☑ "When you've had too much" of the "froufrou" dining scene and "want a beer in wine country", come on down and belly up to the bar of this "funky", "kick-back joint" in "tiny" Geyserville where "Sonoma County locals" queue up for 'cue even though it's "nothing amazing."

GIRL & THE FIG, THE   22 | 20 | 20 | $38 |

110 W. Spain St. (1st St.), Sonoma, 707-938-3634;
www.thegirlandthefig.com

☑ A "must-hit" for many at the "end of a day of wine tasting", Sondra Bernstein's "quaint" Sonoma bistro offers "something for everyone" off its "inspired" French menu ("if you like figs – wow") and wine list sampled via "creative flights"; the room itself is "inviting", but fair weather permits seating outside on the "delightful" patio; N.B. the short-lived Petaluma branch is no longer.

Glen Ellen Inn Restaurant　　▽ 20 | 20 | 20 | $39
13670 Arnold Dr. (Warm Springs Rd.), Glen Ellen, 707-996-6409;
www.glenelleninn.com
◪ Owned by a husband-and-wife team, this "cozy country place" in Glen Ellen serves "innovative" and "eye-pleasing" Cal-Fusion fare that can be sampled à la carte or on the "amazing" Saturday night tasting menu; although some folks' meals have been of "variable" success, optimists claim it's presently "working its way up"; N.B. creek-side cottages house guests who can't bear to leave.

GORDON'S　　　　　　　24 | 17 | 17 | $27
6770 Washington St. (Madison St.), Yountville,
707-944-8246
■ In what's perhaps Yountville's most "poorly kept secret", this "funky, rustic-casual" American cafe harbors a "world-class" chef who creates "out-of-sight" breakfast pastries and desserts; insiders acclaim the "hard-to-get-into" Friday-only dinners but warn "if you're in the wine biz, don't come here on a bad hair day because you're guaranteed to see someone you know" among the "non-touristy" crowd.

Green Valley Cafe ⊠　　　▽ 18 | 13 | 18 | $28
1310 Main St. (Hunt Ave.), St. Helena, 707-963-7088;
www.greenvalleycafe.com
■ "Hearty, classic Northern Italian cuisine" is on hand at this "intimate little bistro in St. Helena"; "friendly service and friendly prices" make it "favored by locals" (you might "meet your favorite winemaker" here), and though it's not fancy – the "small, tight space" has a "jeans-and-boots atmosphere" – it "hits the spot after a day of tiring wine-country touring."

HANA JAPANESE RESTAURANT   25 15 19 $38
Doubletree Plaza, 101 Golf Course Dr. (Roberts Lake Rd.), Rohnert Park, 707-586-0270; www.hanajapanese.com
☑ His shopping-mall "surroundings are uninspired" but his cuisine is anything but, rave Rohnert Park rangers about chef-owner Ken Tominaga, aka "the master Japanese chef of Northern California", who "masterfully prepares" some of "the freshest sushi in Sonoma" and cooked "European-influenced dishes" too; sit at the "black-lacquered" "bar and have him prepare something for you."

Harmony Club   ▽ 21 24 19 $42
Ledson Hotel, 480 First St. E. (Napa St.), Sonoma, 707-996-9779; www.ledsonhotel.com
■ The joint is jumpin' at this "handsome" new eatery/club overlooking the Sonoma Plaza; the kitchen prepares an Eclectic selection of "small plates that sparkle" – served on equally dazzling "fancy, exquisite china with grand silver utensils" – while the bar (doing double duty as a tasting room) pours predominantly Ledson wines ("since they own the place"); be prepared for "pricey" tabs and some noise from the "live music" that rollicks the room nightly.

Hurley's Restaurant & Bar   ▽ 18 19 18 $35
6518 Washington St. (Yount St.), Yountville, 707-944-2345; www.hurleysrestaurant.com
☑ You can dine "without breaking the bank" at this Yountville "locals' hangout" where the "well-chosen, limited" Cal-Med menu includes "interesting wild game dishes"; alas, the "gorgeous high ceilings and tile flooring" create a din, and given the "so-so service" and "inconsistent" eats, the hostile huff it's "not worth the trouble."

Jimtown Store   21 19 18 $15
6706 Hwy. 128 (1 mi. east of Russian River), Healdsburg, 707-433-1212; www.jimtown.com
■ When near Healdsburg, "Harley riders, cyclists and locals" alike stop for the "not-your-ordinary deli" delights

served at this shop (no indoor tables, but there is a "tree-lined patio"); crammed with "novelty items", its "funky country-store atmosphere" – the building dates from 1893 – attracts as much attention as its "inventive" sandwiches, "delicious" tapenades and the "cheerful crew"; N.B. closes at 5 PM.

JOHN ASH & CO.   24 | 25 | 23 | $53

Vintners Inn, 4330 Barnes Rd. (River Rd.), Santa Rosa, 707-527-7687; www.johnashrestaurant.com

■ "Quietly romantic", this "spacious" "Santa Rosa standard" – "tucked away in an inn" – "may be the most beautiful place in Sonoma County" ("get a table overlooking the vineyards" for maximum impact); though lacking a little "variety", the Cal cuisine is "impeccable", the "wine list impressive" and the service is "polished without ever feeling stuffy"; small wonder some sigh "I'm just sorry that I never made it sooner."

JULIA'S KITCHEN   23 | 18 | 19 | $44

COPIA, 500 First St. (bet. Silverado Trail & Soscol Ave.), Napa, 707-265-5700; www.copia.org

◪ "How can any place live up to being named after Julia Child?" – well, it can start by taking "hand-picked, fresher-than-fresh vegetables from the COPIA gardens" and using them in "inventive", "beautifully presented" Cal-French dishes to be delivered by "surprisingly pleasant staffers"; dissenters profess "disappointment", especially in the "industrial atmosphere", but if this "Napa secret" "doesn't knock your socks off, it will at least loosen your shoes."

K&L Bistro   ▽ 25 | 19 | 21 | $41

119 S. Main St. (Bodega Hwy./Hwy. 12), Sebastopol, 707-823-6614

■ For some "French fare with flair" in Sebastopol, surveyors stop by this *petit* place proffering "honest" "bistro classics" and a "very sharp wine list"; its combination of "big-town food and neighborhood feel" is "worth the drive", even if the digs are a bit "nondescript."

KENWOOD
23 | 20 | 21 | $41

9900 Sonoma Hwy./Hwy. 12 (Warm Springs Rd.), Kenwood, 707-833-6326; www.kenwoodrestaurant.com

☑ "The noise level's deafening, but the food's delightful" at this Kenwood veteran surrounded by "vineyards and killer views"; "local winemakers are regulars", commandeering a "table on the terrace" that's "meant for lingering over one more glass of wine" after a French–New American meal that "hodgepodge"-like hops from duck to tapioca pudding.

LASALETTE
24 | – | 24 | $41

Sonoma Plaza, 452 First St. E. (bet. Napa & Spain Sts.), Sonoma, 707-938-1927; www.lasalette-restaurant.com

■ Recently relocated to Sonoma Plaza post-*Survey,* this family-run favorite furnishes loyal locals with a "down-to-earth" taste of the Lisbon table "without the travel"; the "welcoming" staff makes "spot-on recommendations" off the "intriguing" menu and the "superb", "almost all Portuguese" wine list (with a "dizzying selection of ports").

LA TOQUE
27 | 24 | 27 | $93

1140 Rutherford Rd. (Hwy. 29), Rutherford, 707-963-9770; www.latoque.com

■ From the "exquisite" "menus du jour" to the suggested "dress code" to the "serene" room, this Rutherford refuge "is French in every classic sense of the word, and yet it's definitely Napa Valley" with "minimal pretension"; "great" as the Gallic gastronomy is, "what really shines is the service", from the sommelier who "recommends wineries to visit" to chef-owner "Ken Frank himself" who "comes out to shave the truffles" on your dinner, if you're lucky enough to be there "in January, when they're featured."

LEDFORD HOUSE
23 | 23 | 23 | $45

3000 N. Hwy. 1 (Spring Grove Rd.), Albion, 707-937-0282; www.ledfordhouse.com

■ Day-trippers find "heaven on Hwy. 1" at this "favorite" "Mendocino coast establishment"; angelic "husband-

and-wife team" Tony and Lisa Greer "do a wonderful job of making everyone feel as if they're guests in their home", one where she prepares "creative" Cal-Med menus enlivened by "live jazz each evening"; surveyors also shout hosannas for the unrivalled "ocean-sunset views from the bar" ("if there's no fog"; otherwise, case snuggling up to the "welcome fireplace" will have to do).

LITTLE RIVER INN   23 | 23 | 24 | $39
Little River Inn, 7901 N. Hwy. 1 (Little River Airport Rd.), Little River, 707-937-5942; www.littleriverinn.com
■ "There's nothing little about this gem" in Little River, where there's "actually two eating facilities", both with "exceptional service"; the Garden Dining Room, with "fine" Cal food, a "lovely lit garden view and outrageous flower arrangements", caters to tourists celebrating "special occasions"; the "casual, lively" Ole's Whale Watching Bar, sporting "killer ocean" vistas and pub grub, is the locals' preferred perch to "see whales and drink like a fish."

Lucy's   ∇ 18 | 16 | 14 | $32
6948 Sebastopol Ave. (bet. Main St. & Petaluma Ave.), Sebastopol, 707-829-9713
◪ This "wholesome, eco-friendly alternative kind of cafe" is "enormously popular" with the Sebastopol set for "a simple meal"; despite a full Cal-Med menu, a fresh-baked pizza "out of the brick ovens" "is the best thing here"; "service is chaotic", but it's about "the only non-dive bar in town where you can get a decent drink with decent food", "so it all evens out."

MACCALLUM HOUSE   23 | 20 | 21 | $43
MacCallum House Inn, 45020 Albion St. (bet. Kasten & Lansing Sts.), Mendocino, 707-937-5763; www.maccallumhouse.com
◪ A grand ol' historic inn in Mendocino Village that "exudes" "late 19th-century charm", with a warren of "quaint", "intimate" "odd-shaped rooms" in which to

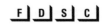
enjoy longtime chef Alan Kantor's "intelligently prepared, perfectly seasoned" Cal cuisine; the presence of "new owners" hasn't manifested itself in the dining room – guests joke "you need the olive oil tasting appetizer to slide into the small tables" – but "hopefully they'll perk up the service."

MADRONA MANOR
25 | 27 | 24 | $61

Madrona Manor Inn, 1001 Westside Rd. (W. Dry Creek Rd.), Healdsburg, 707-433-4231; www.madronamanor.com

■ "Take your date" to this historic Healdsburg landmark (built 1881), the "perfect place to be with someone you love who loves fine food"; "service is professional, yet warm" whether you're enjoying the "sophisticated, well-prepared" New American–French bistro cuisine on the "lovely" terrace or in the "elegant dining room"; those carried away by romance suggest "renting one of their lovely suites."

MANZANITA
22 | 18 | 20 | $44

336 Healdsburg Ave. (North St.), Healdsburg, 707-433-8111

◪ A "menu that highlights seasonal ingredients" (plus "great wood-burning oven pizza"), a "bartender who knows his wines" and servers who are "really good folks" make this Mediterranean "probably Healdsburg's most underrated restaurant" to fans; "not bad, but there are better in town" retort foes, who cite a "cold atmosphere" and "uncreative" vittles.

Market
21 | 20 | 21 | $33

1347 Main St. (bet. Adam & Spring Sts.), St. Helena, 707-963-3799; www.marketsthelena.com

◪ The "professional staff, warm decor", plus one of the "most reasonably priced wine lists" around, ensure a "perfect balance of price, place and people" at this "wine-country winner"; its traditional American eats make a "nice break from all the haute cuisine" in Napa Valley – though since it's "comfort food as executed by a world-class chef"

(Douglas Keane, ex Jardinière, to be precise), clearly "this is not your mother's mac 'n' cheese."

MARTINI HOUSE 25 | 26 | 23 | $53

1245 Spring St. (bet. Main & Oak Sts.), St. Helena, 707-963-2233; www.martinihouse.com

■ "I wanted to move in but was only able to stay for lunch" sums up the sentiment inspired by St. Helena's "extremely romantic" ("complete with blazing fireplace"), "converted Craftsman house"; "always creative", Todd Humphries' "terrific" New American cuisine "perfectly complements the incredible wine list" and "superb" namesake cocktails brought by an "enthusiastic staff"; in short, "sorta spendy, but worth it" for an "over-the-top" experience.

MEADOWOOD GRILL 22 | 22 | 24 | $48

Meadowood Resort, 900 Meadowood Ln. (Howell Mountain Rd., off Silverado Trail), St. Helena, 707-963-3646; www.meadowood.com

■ Whether "you're staying at the hotel" or just "stargazing" at the A-list regulars, this St. Helena Cal with a country-lodge setting can be ideal "for a romantic and relaxed" meal, thanks to the exhaustive all-Napa wine list, "first-rate service" and "lovely patio" "overlooking the golf course" and croquet lawns; P.S. the post-*Survey* arrival of chef Vincent Nattress, who has revamped the "typical grill-oriented menu", may outdate the Food score.

Mendo Bistro ▽ 23 | 16 | 19 | $32

The Company Store, 301 N. Main St., 2nd fl. (Redwood Ave.), Fort Bragg, 707-964-4974; www.mendobistro.com

◪ Chef-owner Nicholas Petti's "goofy hat makes the papers" and his "crab cakes win the awards", but his "cavernous" Fort Bragg bistro has "developed a loyal following" as a "neighborhood restaurant that overachieves"; accompanied by an all-Mendo wine list, the New American–Med menu lets "you choose how you want your meat cooked and sauced"; the "iffy service" is nothing to bragg about, though.

Mirepoix 🕱 ▽ 26 | 18 | 25 | $46
275 Windsor River Rd. (Bell Rd.), Windsor, 707-838-0162
■ "Some of the best food" in Sonoma County can be had –
as long as you "make reservations" – at this "homey" New
American–New French in Windsor that's "worth the detour"
off Hwy. 101; it's "small enough" that "you might get to meet
the chef" and be treated to "excellent, attentive service"
(that happily replenishes the "platters of heavenly flatbread"
accompanying the meal); they'll also waive the corkage
fee on any Sonoma wine not offered from their tiny cellar.

Mixx Restaurant 🕱 21 | 19 | 19 | $39
135 Fourth St. (Davis St.), Santa Rosa, 707-573-1344;
www.mixxrestaurant.com
☑ "Great food" and even "better desserts" (courtesy of co-
owner/pastry chef Kathleen Berman) make this "somewhat
funky" Californian that "fits the mood" of "quirky Railroad
Square" "worth visiting regularly"; adventurous eaters,
however, wish they would mixx it up a bit, muttering that
the menu has "no imagination."

Model Bakery ▽ 22 | 11 | 13 | $12
1357 Main St. (bet. Adams & Spring Sts.), St. Helena,
707-963-8192; www.themodelbakery.com
■ "Who needs Starbucks when you have" this retro-looking
"St. Helena institution" servicing "the elite of Napa Valley";
granted, it's just a "walk-in, order your stuff, walk-out
bakery", but that stuff ("killer cookies", brick-oven "pizza to
die for" and "fabulous grilled panini") provides a delectable
"high-carb start" or "stop in-between winery tastings."

Monti's Rotisserie & Bar – | – | – | M
Montgomery Village Shopping Center, 714 Village Ct.
(Parker Hill Rd.), Santa Rosa, 707-568-4404
Restaurateurs Mark and Terri Stark, the duo behind Willi's
Wine Bar, offer *petit* plates as well as family-style platters
at their newest venture at the Montgomery Village Shopping
Center; the homey farmhouse-inspired decor is matched

by an equally rustic Med menu, while their signature eclectic wine program features pours in many sizes.

Moosse Cafe   20 16 17 $34
Blue Heron Inn, 390 Kasten St. (Albion St.), Mendocino, 707-937-4323; www.theblueheron.com
✇ Situated in the Blue Heron Inn, this casual Cal cafe gets "Mendocino insiders'" vote as a "must-stop for lunch", thanks to "imaginative, delicious salads and sandwiches" and an "enchanted garden with a glimpse of the sea" visible from the "quirky", "intimate" interior; "very slow" staffers, however, have caused the Service score to sink.

MUSTARDS GRILL   24 18 21 $39
7399 St. Helena Hwy./Hwy. 29 (Washington St.), Yountville, 707-944-2424; www.mustardsgrill.com
■ "There is a reason that this place is still so hard to get into": celebrity chef/co-owner Cindy Pawlcyn is "at her best" at this "country roadhouse–like" Napa New American that's perfect "when you've had fusion up to here" and just want "down-home cooking with a gourmet touch"; it's a bit loud, but the signature "Mongolian pork chop is worth sitting next to a jet engine for", and the servers are "jolly people."

Napa General Store   ∇ 18 14 14 $21
500 Main St. (5th St.), Napa, 707-259-0762;
www.napageneralstore.com
✇ "Unpretentious yet delicious (a difficult combo in Napa)", this "informal" "self-service" cafe within a gourmet food shop is "good for the odd" midday hour when you want to grab a "quick bite" of glorified deli and "watch the river roll by" from the deck; N.B. new chef Nam Phan (ex Slanted Door) now offers Pacific Rim small plates on weekends.

Napa Valley Grille   20 19 19 $39
Washington Sq., 6795 Washington St. (Madison St.), Yountville, 707-944-8686; www.napavalleygrille.com
✇ Surveyors are split on this old "reliable" "right in Downtown Yountville": certainly, the "nice patio" is a

"great place for an outdoor" meal and you can feast on the "fine" Cal cuisine (including "desserts that could replace anti-depressants") "and still come home with your wallet intact"; but critics decry a "corporate food and service" mentality (it's "part of a chain"), shrugging it's "too standard to be worth a stop in Napa."

Napa Valley Wine Train 17 24 20 $64
1275 McKinstry St. (bet. 1st St. & Soscol Ave.), Napa, 800-427-4124; www.winetrain.com
☑ "Go during the daytime" "so you really get to see the beauty of the Napa Valley" while riding a "restored" train, urge those who are on board with this meals-on-wheels adventure; the Cal cuisine is "surprisingly palatable", though "of course not gourmet level", and the service "professional"; "certainly, it's a tourist trap", but a nice "one-time experience" as well.

955 Ukiah ∇ 21 19 21 $41
955 Ukiah St. (School St.), Mendocino, 707-937-1955; www.955restaurant.com
■ Yes, the "funky" '70s decor of this "tucked-away-off-the-beaten-path Mendocino Village secret" "takes you back" – but what brings you back is the "delicious seasonal" New American–New French fare fashioned "from local farms' and fishermen's" wares that's "cooked with love" and served "with panache" by "gracious, informative servers" who "even have suggestions about events going on" around the county.

Osake ⌺ ∇ 22 18 18 $35
2446 Patio Ct. (Farmer's Ln.), Santa Rosa, 707-542-8282; www.garychus.com
■ There's just "no stopping Gary Chu" who, when not running his eponymous Chinese, is "often here behind the sushi counter with fast hands and a hearty laugh", preparing "outrageous" "fusion rolls" and other "eclectic" Cal-Japanese dishes; his "pleasing personality"

pervades the "friendly", "well-designed" Santa Rosa space that includes a 250-gallon decorative "fish tank in the entrance bar area."

Pangaea   ▽ 22 | 18 | 19 | $40

39165 Shoreline Hwy./S. Hwy. 1 (eastern side of the Hwy.), Gualala, 707-884-9669

■ Having moved from Pt. Arena to Downtown Gualala, this Mendocino coast sleeper is "better than ever" swear supporters of its self-billed "zaftig" Cal cuisine – "eclectic, robust" offerings like a "bittersweet chocolate cake", washed down with organic and biodynamic bottlings; the owners have made the new surroundings "in the middle of nowhere" more inviting, with "a bright mix of Provençal charm and urbane funk."

Pearl ☒   ▽ 22 | 17 | 22 | $29

1339 Pearl St. (bet. Franklin & Polk Sts.), Napa, 707-224-9161; www.therestaurantpearl.com

■ This "quaint" Downtown Napa joint is "the place locals hope you don't find out about" – "where winemakers go" when they want "terrific food but with none of the fanfare of the up-valley dining temples"; the "friendly" husband-and-wife owners "do a bang-up job" "in the kitchen and on the floor", serving Cal comfort food "like mom used to make if she were a heckuva good cook"; P.S. the "delicious oyster" selection is considered the pearl of the menu.

Père Jeanty   21 | 21 | 19 | $43

6725 Washington St. (Madison St.), Yountville, 707-945-1000; www.perejeanty.com

☑ Francophiles who travel for a taste of chef-entrepreneur Philippe Jeanty's French food now have this "fun new option", complete with a communal table and antique Gallic bric-a-brac; *la différence* here is that this large Yountville outpost's "interesting" Provençal menu features "lighter fare" – seafood, pizzas, "even a great hamburger"; comparison shoppers say it's not up to "sibling Bistro

Jeanty" (particularly the "unpolished staff") but concede "it's a good second choice."

Piatti　　　　　　　　　18 | 19 | 18 | $34 |

El Dorado Hotel, 405 First St. W. (Spain St.), Sonoma, 707-996-2351
6480 Washington St. (Oak Circle), Yountville, 707-944-2070
www.piatti.com

☑ A "cheerful chain" with branches in Sonoma and Yountville, these "kid-friendly" spots are "not like mama's, but good"; a "cozy atmosphere" and "solid Italian food" win over many, especially since you can "enjoy your meal without breaking the bank"; but service that "can be, at times, indifferent" and "cookie-cutter" choices leave some saying "ho-hum."

Pilar ☒　　　　　　　　　– | – | – | M |

807 Main St. (3rd St.), Napa, 707-252-4474

Named for the Food Network personality Pilar Sanchez, working with co-chef/husband Didier Lenders, this new eatery near the Napa River is all about the wine country, from the local, seasonally driven Cal menu to the dining room's focal visual, a woodblock triptych ('The Farmer', 'The Winemaker', 'The Cook'); however, the actual vino list, which is categorized by varietal, carries both U.S. producers (listed on one side) and their foreign counterparts (on the other).

Pinot Blanc　　　　　　　20 | 23 | 21 | $47 |

641 Main St. (Grayson Ave.), St. Helena, 707-963-6191;
www.patinagroup.com

☑ Set in the heart of St. Helena, this send-up of a Provençal country inn with a "posh" interior and "great alfresco dining" is a "gorgeous setting" for a "relaxing" "sit-down lunch while on the prowl for wine", enhanced by "service at your choice of pace" and a "broad by-the-glass" list; however, considering that this pricey Cal–New French is "part of the Splichal empire in LA", "it should be great, but it just misses."

Pizza Azzurro ⌧   ▽ 21 | 12 | 17 | $20

1400 Second St. (Franklin St.), Napa, 707-255-5552
◪ "For a quick meal in Downtown Napa", this pie shop offers something more than your "ordinary pepperoni pizza stop"; though the setting may be "rather utilitarian" and the servers "pretty amateur", the "terrific thin-crust" pies crowned with "unique gourmet toppings" and the wines from "local boutique wineries" "overshadow any complaint one might have with the decor or service."

Pizzeria Tra Vigne   20 | 18 | 17 | $23

(fka Vitte)
Inn at Southbridge, 1016 Main St. (Pope St.), St. Helena, 707-967-9999; www.pizzeriatravigne.com
■ After years of being known as 'that pizza joint run by Tra Vigne', this St. Helena Italian now officially bears the mother ship's name; the menu also offers pasta and piadine ("salad wrapped in flatbread"), as well as a "great wine list (for a pizzeria)" or "free corkage" if you bring your own; TVs and a pool table make it "a favorite to take children to."

RAVENOUS   23 | 18 | 20 | $38

420 Center St. (North St.), Healdsburg, 707-431-1770
◪ This "quintessential neighborhood cafe", set in a "charming" "little white" cottage near "the Plaza stores", has "become a destination in its own right"; "lunch is for sure a hit", to the extent "they run out of half" of the Cal menu "by the end of the day", but dinner "in the garden" or in the dim, "intimate" interior is rather "romantic"; however, "the name describes the condition" many get into, due to "quirky service"; P.S. heartsick Healdsburgers "miss [late sibling] Ravenette next to the Raven Theater."

Rendezvous Inn & Restaurant   ▽ 25 | 19 | 21 | $43

647 N. Main St. (Bush St.), Fort Bragg, 707-964-8142; www.rendezvousinn.com
◪ "An auberge in Fort Bragg? – well, not really", but that's what "passionate" chef-owner Kim Badenhop's

"outstanding" New French aspires to be; his "creative" dishes, each "complemented by an amazing wine" suggestion, are "absolutely impeccable", and they're served by an "eloquent staff"; some new gardens may mollify those who say the 1897 B&B "needs help in the looks department"; otherwise, a trip here "makes a weekend on the Mendocino coast perfect."

RESTAURANT AT STEVENSWOOD, THE
26 | 24 | 26 | $53

Stevenswood Lodge, 8211 Shoreline Hwy./Hwy. 1 (2 mi. south of Mendocino), Little River, 707-937-2810; www.stevenswood.com
■ "Chef Marc Dym deserves to swim in a much bigger pond", so Little River "couldn't be luckier to have him" cooking up "beautifully presented" Mediterranean cuisine that's "always a half-step ahead of others"; "everything [else] is superlative" at this "stunner", too, from the "elegant", "intimate setting" to the highly "helpful waiters."

Restaurant 301
▽ 22 | 22 | 24 | $44

Carter House Inn, 301 L St. (3rd St.), Eureka, 707-444-8062; www.carterhouse.com
■ Explorers who make "the detour off 101" shout Eureka – what a "surprisingly" "high-class" establishment "so far up the North Coast"; the high-ceilinged Victorian room provides ambiance for the garden-fresh (from the inn's own garden) New American–New French fare that occasionally "overreaches" but often is "outstanding"; the "educated staff has helpful ideas on wine pairings" from the 3,800-label cellar, but also "knows how to point you to a bargain."

Ristorante Allegria
▽ 20 | 23 | 21 | $36

1026 First St. (Main St.), Napa, 707-254-8006; www.ristoranteallegria.com
◪ Endowed with a "killer location" – a Downtown Napa "beautiful, restored old bank building" – this Italian "fittingly pays a dividend" in the shape of sake cocktails,

"attentive service" and quite "good food"; however, the sound "echoes insanely on busy nights", and skeptics sigh that while the sophomore "started off with a well-deserved bang", it's "sort of settled down into a less-spectacular version"; P.S. high rollers should "ask for the vault room for special occasions."

Rutherford Grill   21 19 20 $34

1180 Rutherford Rd. (Hwy. 29), Rutherford, 707-963-1792;
www.houstons.com

◪ "The scene is a who's-who of the Napa Valley wine industry" (maybe because they can bring their own with "no cork .ge fee") at Rutherford's "down-homey grill house" where "unhurried servers" deliver American eats that range from "knife-and-fork ribs" to "spectacular teriyaki ostrich"; and if it "seems like a Houston's", well, that's because they own it; P.S. reservations are now accepted, which may ease the "long waits."

Santé   ▽ 20 21 22 $48

Sonoma Mission Inn & Spa, 100 Boyes Blvd. (Sonoma Hwy.),
Sonoma, 707-939-2415; www.fairmont.com

◪ "To see the impressive Sonoma Mission Inn" is reason alone for a visit, but those who've "been pampered all day at the spa" also laud the Cal fare ("this is the way all health food should taste") offered by "attentive, yet discreet service" in this "posh", "peaceful" place; the recent arrival of chef Bruno Tison (ex NYC's The Plaza Hotel) may smooth out the "uneven" edges some cite.

SANTI   24 20 22 $41

21047 Geyserville Ave. (Hwy. 128), Geyserville, 707-857-1790;
www.tavernasanti.com

■ When "everything in Healdsburg is booked up", take your wine-country visitors to this Geyserville "sleeper" – or better yet, "send them here first", as it's "one of the few out there" "that really tastes like Italy", with "lovingly prepared" and "graciously served" "soul food" from the northern regions that can be enjoyed in the "cozy inside" or on "a lovely garden out back"; the wine list features the "familiar" along with "new things to try."

Sassafras Restaurant & Wine Bar　▽ 20 ⎮ 17 ⎮ 21 ⎮ $33 ⎮
Santa Rosa Business Park, 1229 N. Dutton Ave. (College Ave.), Santa Rosa, 707-578-7600
◪ While the Santa Rosa "business park setting is a bit off-putting, once inside" customers "run to the wine bar" for "fun and educational flights" from the born-in-the-USA cellar at this vino and food "pairing paradise"; "new chef-owner Jack Mitchell has improved the quality" of the New American eats, but "that ratty decor has got to go."

Sea Ranch Lodge Restaurant　▽ 18 ⎮ 19 ⎮ 17 ⎮ $43 ⎮
Sea Ranch Lodge, 60 Sea Walk Dr. (Hwy. 1), Sea Ranch, 707-785-2371; www.searanchlodge.com
■ Perched on the northern Sonoma coastline, this "remote, romantic" resort restaurant is a "welcome refuge off Highway 1"; "killer views of the ocean" lend themselves to "leisurely dinners" of locally-caught seafood and "monthly winemaker dinners that are a treat"; however, old ranch hands prefer watching the sunset and "having a drink" "in the glassed-in sun room", which offers a "good bar menu."

Seaweed Café　　　　　　　–⎮ –⎮ –⎮ M ⎮
(fka Seaweed House)
1580 Eastshore Rd. (Hwy. 1), Bodega Bay, 707-875-2700; www.seaweedcafe.com
"Surely one of the best in Bodega Bay" say the few who know this miniscule, mustard-colored cafe where French-born chef/co-owner Jackie Martine relies predominantly on local Sonoma larders to create his "eclectic", all-organic Californian version of 'coastal cuisine', which is paired with an exclusive Sonoma wine list (anything grown west of Highway 101); N.B. the prix-fixe dinner is served Friday–Monday only.

Sharon's By the Sea   ▽ 20 | 13 | 18 | $31

*Noyo Harbor, 32096 N. Harbor Dr. (Hwy. 1), Fort Bragg,
707-962-0680*
*Hill House Inn, 10701 Palette Dr. (Lansing St.), Mendocino,
707-937-3200*
www.sharonsbythesea.com

■ This "hidden" "harborside hangout" perched on the
pier in Fort Bragg offers "the best bang for the buck on
the North Coast" – "and such a tasty bang" it is, with its
"always good" Italianate seafood; the interior has been
expanded, but "outside on the deck" under the bridge is
preferred to "just watch the seagulls", "seals at play" and
fishermen reeling in what's likely to be on your plate;
P.S. "Sharon's just started cooking at the Hill House Inn
in Mendocino Village."

Sonoma Meritage & Oyster Bar   ▽ 22 | 18 | 20 | $38

*522 Broadway (bet. E. Napa & Patten Sts.), Sonoma, 707-938-9430;
www.sonomameritage.com*

◪ Though the bivalves are "as fresh as can be", "don't be
fooled – this oyster bar serves one heck of an osso buco"
or whatever French–Northern Italian dishes the chef is
making that day; "generous portions" and an "excellent
wine list" featuring local and imported selections make it
ideal for "lunch just off the Sonoma Square"; doubters
who say "a new location might help" the dark digs will
delight in a move, scheduled in September at press time,
to 165 Napa Street.

Sonoma Saveurs   ▽ 26 | 20 | 20 | $32

*487 First St. W. (bet. Napa & Spain Sts.), Sonoma, 707-996-7007;
www.sonomasaveurs.com*

■ "Get ready to say ooh-la-la" at this "brilliant new" bistro/
wine bar/store just off the Sonoma Square; it serves
"lovingly prepared classic French fare" along with locally
made "picnic food", but it's already known as "the home of
the perfect foie gras", served in an adobe-walled room
that's "cozy or cramped, depending on your viewpoint."

St. Orres
▽ 24 24 23 $54

36601 Shoreline Hwy./Hwy. 1 (2 mi. north of Gualala), Gualala, 707-884-3303; www.saintorres.com

☑ Chef Rosemary Campiformio puts her "little candied" "heart in the salads" and everything else she prepares on her "whimsical" prix fixe dinners in a Gualala bed-and-breakfast "way out-of-the-way up the coast"; saints say "it's a sin not to go when she's cooking" just to sample the Cal "menu of all things hunted – shark, boar, venison and more [served] under the onion-domed dining room's hanging gardens"; but devils declare the "contrived cuisine" "could use updating."

SYRAH ☒
24 18 22 $44

205 Fifth St. (Davis St.), Santa Rosa, 707-568-4002; www.syrahbistro.com

☑ Centrally located in "historic Railroad Square", this Cal-French bistro "is becoming the place to go in Santa Rosa" for an "intimate dinner" at "reasonable prices", featuring a "constantly changing menu", "fantastic wine list" and "friendly service"; chef-owner Josh Silvers' passion is evident whether he's in the "open kitchen that's fun to watch" or "chatting with customers", and enables many to overlook the "industrial feeling" of the dining room and the outdoor seating in an "office-building atrium."

TAYLOR'S AUTOMATIC REFRESHER
22 14 16 $15

933 Main St. (bet. Charter Oak Ave. & Pope St.), St. Helena, 707-963-3486; www.taylorsrefresher.com

■ "Not your father's roadside hamburger stand" – more like "a Dairy Queen that died and went to heaven", this "iconic" "1950s" "walk-up" diner in St. Helena is "a junk-food lover's dream", flipping classics like "blue-cheese burgers so messy they drip down your arm" along with "seared ahi" and killer vinos; "it's always jammed" and "a little overpriced" but still "one of the cheaper places" in the area.

TERRA
26 24 25 $60

1345 Railroad Ave. (bet. Adams & Hunt Sts.), St. Helena, 707-963-8931; www.terrarestaurant.com

■ "Trust your culinary fortunes to Hiro Sone and his wife, Lissa Doumani", who deliver "all the bang-for-big-bucks" with an "exquisite", "flawlessly executed" New American (with Southern French and Northern Italian influences) menu at their Napa Valley "destination" housed in a "beautiful old" fieldstone building; the "wine list is more like a dictionary" and the "gracious" staff so "knowledgeable it was as if they were in the kitchen preparing the food."

TRA VIGNE
24 25 22 $48

1050 Charter Oak Ave. (Hwy. 29), St. Helena, 707-963-4444; www.travignerestaurant.com

■ A stop at St. Helena's "quintessential Napa Valley restaurant" is like being "wined and dined at a private Tuscan villa" by "attentive" hosts who "know every wine and every vineyard"; dazzled devotees are undecided whether the "excellent" Italian fare "enhances the sun-dappled courtyard setting, or the other way around", but it's moot for most who can't think of a better way "to spend a romantic afternoon before hitting the wineries"; P.S. the "bar is a great place" to "drop in without a reservation" and "meet local vintners."

Tuscany
17 21 17 $35

1005 First St. (Main St.), Napa, 707-258-1000

◪ For Northern Italian "country-style cuisine" "with a wine-country accent", *amici* aver this Napa spot "can deliver" "really good food" and "fine service", but locals lament that "it's devolved into a tourist mill" with "unpredictable" fare that's "not worth the wait" or the "noise during the summer"; still, many are drawn by the "regional decor" – think "weathered wood beams", "flower boxes" and "French doors that open up to the warm weather."

Underwood Bar & Bistro   ▽ 21 22 18 $39
9113 Graton Rd. (Edison St.), Graton, 707-823-7023
■ "You'd swear you were in a great NY bistro", not "the middle of rural Sonoma", at this bustling "cosmopolitan" Graton spot fans consider to be one "of the best in the area"; the Southern Med fare is "well prepared" and the "portions are generous, even on the tapas plates", but the "lively" "bar's the thing here", and has become a late-night "social spot" for locals.

Uva Trattoria & Bar   ▽ 21 18 20 $31
1040 Clinton St. (Main St.), Napa, 707-255-6646;
www.uvatrattoria.com
■ Though it's centrally located near the opera house and shopping, this "pleasant and hip" Southern Italian "date place" is something of a "secret of Downtown dining" in Napa; "finding it can be a challenge", but locals laud its "nice, fresh" fare and wines at "reasonable prices" and staff that treats you "like a royal subject"; P.S. many "dishes come in both small and full-size portions."

Victorian Gardens   ▽ 24 26 27 $75
The Inn at Victorian Gardens, 14409 Shoreline Hwy./Hwy. 1
(south of Elk, 8 mi. north of Pt. Arena), Manchester, 707-882-3606
■ "Dining with the Zambonis" at their exclusive B&B in Mendocino's Manchester is "like dining in with your best friends" (who happen to live in a "storybook" Victorian house on a 92-acre farm); "you may meet Luciano in the hen house with an axe or in the garden" as he "lovingly prepares" the nightly prix fixe of "homey Italian cuisine", while Pauline can be found in the 16-seat dining room doling out "old-world hospitality."

VILLA CORONA   23 11 16 $14
1138 Main St. (bet. Pope & Spring Sts.), St. Helena, 707-963-7812
3614 Bel Aire Plaza (Trancas St.), Napa, 707-257-8685
◪ "Once you get over the plastic lawn chairs" at these "small and basic" St. Helena and Napa establishments,

you'll appreciate the "delicious", "hearty" and "affordable" Mexican fare that amigos attest is some of "the best in the valley"; the staff is "accommodating" and "takeout is fast when you call ahead", all of which makes this duo a "favorite among locals."

WAPPO BAR BISTRO   23 | 19 | 18 | $36 |
1226 Washington St. (Lincoln Ave.), Calistoga, 707-942-4712;
www.wappobar.com
■ "It's simply divine" to "eat outdoors under the vine-covered arbor" at this "old reliable" in Calistoga offering a "wonderful, inventive" Eclectic menu and "fair-priced" wines, and while "some of the dishes are a bit of a stretch, nothing is poorly done"; the service can be "slow", but the staff is a "hoot", "gladly sharing interesting life stories if your dinner companions get boring."

Wappo Taco   ▽ 22 | 15 | 16 | $22 |
1458 Lincoln Ave. (Fair Way), Calistoga, 707-942-8165
■ The folks behind the globally inspired Wappo Bar Bistro have narrowed their focus with this "inviting" sit-down Mexican in the historic Calistoga Depot serving "flavorful", "ultra-fresh" south-of-the-border *cocina* in a brightly painted tropical interior (hanging chiles, potted palms and a salsa bar) or on an outdoor patio; cervezas, sangria, and agua frescas are the beverages of choice.

Water Street Bistro ⊅   ▽ 23 | 14 | 17 | $19 |
100 Petaluma Blvd. N. (Western Ave.), Petaluma,
707-763-9563
■ "Everything is made from scratch" by chef-owner Stephanie Rastetter at her "cute little cafe" overlooking the Petaluma River, from "creative breakfasts" to "consistently satisfying" French bistro fare; "excellent prices" also make it a sweet spot for your morning meal or "lunch on the way to the wine country", but "alas, she's only open one night a month" for eight-course theme dinners, Friday and Saturday nights in the summer.

WILLI'S SEAFOOD & RAW BAR　25　22　22　$41

403 Healdsburg Ave. (North St.), Healdsburg, 707-433-9191

☑ "A happening place to see and be seen" in Healdsburg, where you can "sit out on the patio, drink a mojito and relax", this "fab" tapas seafooder serves "fresh, fresh" fin fare and "masterfully prepared" small plates (including "imaginative" seviches and some of "the best oysters in town"); "pairing wines is easy and affordable", as they're "all available by the half-bottle" or glass, but frugal finatics fume over the "little dishes" with "big-plate prices."

WILLI'S WINE BAR　24　19　21　$41

Orchard Inn, 4404 Old Redwood Hwy. (River Rd.), Santa Rosa, 707-526-3096; www.williswinebar.net

■ "Creative" international tapas "done to perfection" is the draw of "one of the hottest restaurants" in Santa Rosa, where a "friendly, knowledgeable" staff and a "lovely patio" also contribute to an "extraordinary experience"; oenophiles appreciate that all the wines are available by the taste, glass, half-bottle or bottle; but wallet-watchers warn the "small plates can add up to big dollars."

Willow Wood Market Cafe　▽　23　14　15　$27

9020 Graton Rd. (Edison St.), Graton, 707-522-8372

☑ "Russian River wine folks know" this "complete country charmer" in the "one-horse town" of Graton, an Eclectic "hippie-inspired market/restaurant" that is the "antithesis" of many chichi wine-country competitors; everything is so "fresh" coming out of the "tiny kitchen" ("awesome breakfasts", "excellent soups", "homemade bakery items galore"), and the "casual, whimsical atmosphere" has "lots of soul", excusing the sometimes "apathetic" service.

WINE SPECTATOR GREYSTONE　23　23　21　$47

Culinary Institute of America, 2555 Main St. (Deer Park Rd.), St. Helena, 707-967-1010; www.ciachef.edu

■ Part of the Culinary Institute of America complex, this Cal is "a fun place for foodies" where you can enjoy not only "creative, cutting-edge" cuisine and "superb service", but also "free entertainment as you watch your meal prepared" by professional chefs in the open exhibition kitchen; the "cavernous" dining room "can get very loud", but the "patio is one of the most beautiful spots for lunch in the Valley."

ZAZU   24 | 18 | 22 | $43

3535 Guerneville Rd. (Willowside Rd.), Santa Rosa, 707-523-4814; www.zazurestaurant.com

☑ In Santa Rosa, chef-owners Duskie Estes and John Stewart "run a classic mom-and-pop restaurant" serving "sophisticated yet homey", "consistently excellent" New American–Northern Italian cuisine from an "ever-changing" menu; a "very accommodating staff" works hard to make you "comfortable" in the "roadhouse" setting, even if the noise level "makes it an excellent place to practice lip reading on busy nights."

Zin   21 | 19 | 20 | $37

344 Center St. (North St.), Healdsburg, 707-473-0946; www.zinrestaurant.com

☑ This "informal" "blue-plate" paradise "one street off the town square" is "probably the best dining value in Healdsburg", thanks to "generous portions" of "great American comfort food" and a "super selection of namesake wines"; it's popular with "grape growers" as well as tourists eager to "wind down after a day visiting wineries", and while the service can be "uneven" and the decor is a bit "stark", the "reliable fare" makes up for any number of zins.

Zinsvalley ☒   ∇ 22 | 19 | 21 | $31

Browns Valley Shopping Ctr., 3253 Browns Valley Rd. (bet. Austin & Larkin Sts.), Napa, 707-224-0695; www.zinsvalley.com

■ "Do your zinning here" insist imbibing locals of this "local hangout" "tucked away in Browns Valley" that "deserves to be known by a wider crowd"; not only is "the wine list of

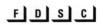

Zinfandels hard-to-beat", but it "matches well" with the "wonderful", affordable New American fare, and the "owners greet you warmly"; all's best savored on the "gorgeous back patio", and "cellar rats" revel in the fact there's "no corkage fee."

ZUZU
23 | 17 | 20 | $33

829 Main St. (bet. 2nd & 3rd Sts.), Napa, 707-224-8555;
www.zuzunapa.com
■ "Tapas are the topic" at this stylish, snug Spaniard just "along the Napa River", where guests "make a fun evening of tasting" "inventive small plates", "mighty fine sangria" and "bottles of little-known gems from Spain that won't break the bank"; but since this "naturally noisy" "social scene" is strictly first-come, first-served, "prepare to wait if you show up" at prime time.

CUISINES

American (New)
Alexis Baking Co.
Bistro Ralph
Boonville Hotel
Brannan's Grill
Café La Haye
Cafe Lolo
Celadon
Cindy's Backstreet
Deuce
Dry Creek Kit.
Duck Club
French Laundry
Fumé Bistro
Kenwood
Madrona Manor
Martini Hse.
Mendo Bistro
Mirepoix
Mustards Grill
955 Ukiah
Rest. 301
Sassafras
Terra
zazu
Zinsvalley

American (Traditional)
BayLeaf Rest.
Chapter & Moon
Gordon's
Market
Rutherford Grill
Taylor's Automatic
Zin

Bakeries
Alexis Baking Co.
Downtown Bakery
Model Bakery

Barbecue
Foothill Cafe
Geyser Smokehse.

Californian
Albion River Inn
Alexander Valley
All Season's Cafe
Applewood Inn
Boonville Hotel
Brix
Cafe Beaujolais
Café La Haye
Calistoga Inn
Carneros
Cindy's Backstreet
Domaine Chandon
Farmhouse Inn
General's Daughter
Glen Ellen Inn
Hurley's Rest.
John Ash & Co.
Julia's Kitchen
Ledford Hse.
Little River Inn
Lucy's
MacCallum Hse.
Madrona Manor
Meadowood Grill
Mixx Rest.
Moosse Cafe

Napa Valley Grille
Napa Valley Train
Osake
Pangaea
Pearl
Pilar
Pinot Blanc
Ravenous
Santé
Seaweed Café
St. Orres
Syrah
Wine Spectator

Chinese
Gary Chu's

Coffee Shops/Diners
Taylor's Automatic

Delis
Jimtown Store

Dessert
Downtown Bakery

Eclectic
Celadon
Harmony Club
Wappo Bar
Willi's Wine Bar
Willow Wood Mkt.

French
Alexander Valley
Angèle
Auberge du Soleil
Cafe Beaujolais
fig cafe
French Laundry

Julia's Kitchen
Kenwood
Sonoma Meritage
Sonoma Saveurs

French (Bistro)
Bistro Jeanty
Bistrot La Poste
Bouchon
Brasserie/Mer
Charcuterie
girl & the fig
K&L Bistro
Père Jeanty
Syrah
Water St. Bistro

French (New)
La Toque
Mirepoix
955 Ukiah
Pinot Blanc
Rendezvous Inn
Rest. 301

Hamburgers
Taylor's Automatic

Italian
(N=Northern; S=Southern)
Belle Arti (S)
Bistro Don Giov.
Cafe Citti (N)
Cena Luna
Cucina Paradiso (S)
Della Santina's (N)
Green Valley Cafe (N)
Piatti
Pizzeria Tra Vigne

Cuisine Index

Rist. Allegria (N)
Santi (N)
Sharon's By Sea
Sonoma Meritage (N)
Tra Vigne
Tuscany (N)
Uva Tratt. (S)
Victorian Garden
zazu (N)

Japanese
(* sushi specialist)
Hana Japanese*
Osake*

Mediterranean
Auberge du Soleil
Chez Felice
Hurley's Rest.
Ledford Hse.
Lucy's
Manzanita
Mendo Bistro
Monti's Rotisserie
Rest. at Stevenswood
Underwood Bar

Mexican
Villa Corona
Wappo Taco

Pacific Rim
Napa General

Pizza
Manzanita
Pizza Azzurro
Pizzeria Tra Vigne

Portuguese
LaSalette

Sandwiches
Downtown Bakery
Jimtown Store

Seafood
Brasserie/Mer
Sea Ranch Lodge
Sharon's By Sea
Willi's Seafood

Small Plates
Cindy's Backstreet
Harmony Club
Underwood Bar
Willi's Seafood
Willi's Wine Bar

Spanish
(* tapas specialist)
Zuzu*

Steakhouses
Cole's Chop Hse.

LOCATIONS

MENDOCINO

Albion
Albion River Inn
Ledford Hse.

Boonville
Boonville Hotel

Eureka
Rest. 301

Fort Bragg
Chapter & Moon
Mendo Bistro
Rendezvous Inn
Sharon's By Sea

Gualala
Pangaea

St. Orres

Little River
Little River Inn
Rest. at Stevenswood

Manchester
Victorian Garden

Mendocino
Cafe Beaujolais
MacCallum Hse.
Moosse Cafe
955 Ukiah
Sharon's By Sea

Sea Ranch
Sea Ranch Lodge

NAPA

Calistoga
All Season's Cafe
Brannan's Grill
Calistoga Inn
Wappo Bar
Wappo Taco

Napa
Alexis Baking Co.
Angèle
BayLeaf Rest.
Belle Arti
Bistro Don Giov.
Celadon
Cole's Chop Hse.

Foothill Cafe
Fumé Bistro
Julia's Kitchen
Napa General
Napa Valley Train
Pearl
Pilar
Pizza Azzurro
Rist. Allegria
Tuscany
Uva Tratt.
Villa Corona
Zinsvalley
Zuzu

Location Index

Petaluma
Cucina Paradiso
Water St. Bistro

Rohnert Park
Hana Japanese

Santa Rosa
Brasserie/Mer
Cafe Lolo
Gary Chu's
John Ash & Co.
Mixx Rest.
Monti's Rotisserie
Osake
Sassafras
Syrah
Willi's Wine Bar
zazu

Sebastopol
K&L Bistro
Lucy's

Sonoma
Bistrot La Poste
Café La Haye
Carneros
Della Santina's
Deuce
General's Daughter
girl & the fig
Harmony Club
LaSalette
Piatti
Santé
Sonoma Meritage
Sonoma Saveurs

Windsor
Chez Felice
Mirepoix

Napa Wineries

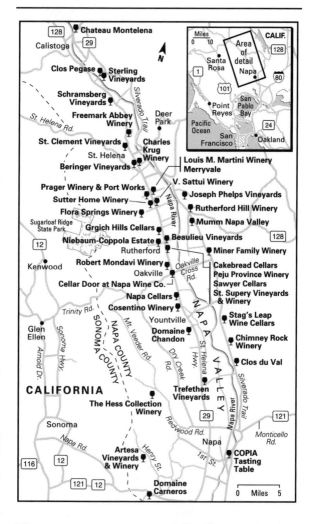

52

Sonoma Wineries

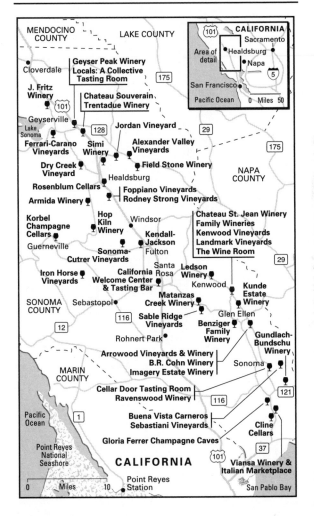

MENDOCINO COUNTY

LAKE COUNTY

CALIFORNIA
Sacramento
Area of detail
Healdsburg
Napa
San Francisco
Pacific Ocean
0 Miles 50

Cloverdale

Geyser Peak Winery
Locals: A Collective
Tasting Room

J. Fritz Winery

Chateau Souverain
Trentadue Winery

Geyserville

Jordan Vineyard

Ferrari-Carano Vineyards

Simi Winery

Alexander Valley Vineyards

Dry Creek Vineyard

Field Stone Winery

Healdsburg

NAPA COUNTY

Rosenblum Cellars

Foppiano Vineyards
Rodney Strong Vineyards

Armida Winery

Korbel Champagne Cellars

Hop Kiln Winery

Windsor

Chateau St. Jean Winery
Family Wineries
Kenwood Vineyards
Landmark Vineyards
The Wine Room

Guerneville

Kendall-Jackson

Sonoma-Cutrer Vineyards

Fulton

Iron Horse Vineyards

California Welcome Center & Tasting Bar

Santa Rosa

Ledson Winery

Kenwood

Kunde Estate Winery

SONOMA COUNTY

Sebastopol

Matanzas Creek Winery

Sable Ridge Vineyards

Glen Ellen

Benziger Family Winery

Gundlach-Bundschu Winery

Rohnert Park

Arrowood Vineyards & Winery
B.R. Cohn Winery
Imagery Estate Winery

Sonoma

MARIN COUNTY

Cellar Door Tasting Room
Ravenswood Winery

Buena Vista Carneros
Sebastiani Vineyards

Cline Cellars

Pacific Ocean

Gloria Ferrer Champagne Caves

Point Reyes National Seashore

CALIFORNIA

Viansa Winery & Italian Marketplace

0 Miles 10

Point Reyes Station

San Pablo Bay

Mendocino Wineries

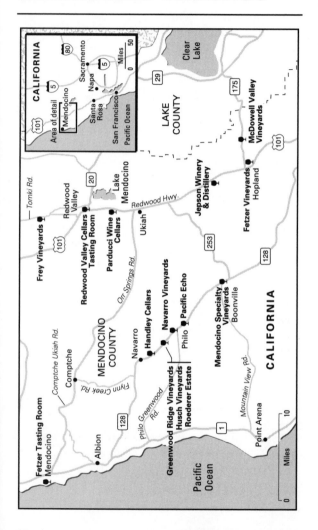

WINERIES & TASTING ROOMS

Napa County

Artesa Vineyards & Winery
1345 Henry Rd., Napa, 707-224-1668;
www.artesawinery.com

Beaulieu Vineyards
1960 St. Helena Hwy., Rutherford, 800-373-5896;
www.bvwines.com

Beringer Vineyards
2000 Main St., St. Helena, 707-963-7115;
www.beringer.com

Cakebread Cellars
8300 St. Helena Hwy., Rutherford, 707-963-5221;
800-588-0298; www.cakebread.com

Cellar Door at Napa Wine Co.
7830-40 St. Helena Hwy., Oakville, 707-944-1710;
800-848-9630; www.napawineco.com

Charles Krug Winery
2800 Main St., St. Helena, 707-967-2200; 800-237-0033;
www.charleskrug.com

Chateau Montelena
1429 Tubbs Ln., Calistoga, 707-942-5105;
www.montelena.com

Chimney Rock Winery
5340 Silverado Trail, Napa, 707-257-2641; 800-257-2641;
www.chimneyrock.com

Clos du Val
5330 Silverado Trail, Napa, 707-259-2225; 800-993-9463;
www.closduval.com

Clos Pegase
1060 Dunaweal Ln., Calistoga, 707-942-4981; 800-366-8583;
www.clospegase.com

COPIA Tasting Table
500 First St., Napa, 707-259-1600; 888-512-6742; www.copia.org

Cosentino Winery
7415 St. Helena Hwy., Yountville, 707-944-1220;
www.cosentinowinery.com

Domaine Carneros
1240 Duhig Rd., Napa, 707-257-0101; www.domaine.com

Domaine Chandon
1 California Dr., Yountville, 707-944-2280; 800-934-3975;
www.chandon.com

Flora Springs Winery
1978 W. Zinfandel Ln., St. Helena, 707-963-5711;
www.florasprings.com

Freemark Abbey Winery
3022 St. Helena Hwy. N., St. Helena, 707-963-9694;
800-963-9698; www.freemarkabbey.com

Grgich Hills Cellars
1829 St. Helena Hwy., Rutherford, 707-963-2784;
800-532-3057; www.grgich.com

Hess Collection Winery, The
4411 Redwood Rd., Napa, 707-255-1144;
www.hesscollection.com

Joseph Phelps Vineyards
200 Taplin Rd., St. Helena, 707-963-2745; 800-707-5789;
www.jpvwines.com

Louis M. Martini Winery
254 St. Helena Hwy., St. Helena, 707-963-2736;
800-321-9463; www.louismartini.com

Merryvale
1000 Main St., St. Helena, 707-963-7777; 800-326-6069;
www.merryvale.com

Miner Family Winery
7850 Silverado Trail, Oakville, 707-944-9500; 800-366-9463;
www.minerwines.com

Mumm Napa Valley
8445 Silverado Trail, Rutherford, 707-967-7700;
www.mummcuveenapa.com

Napa Cellars
7481 St. Helena Hwy., Oakville, 707-944-2565; 800-535-6400;
www.napacellars.com

Niebaum-Coppola Estate
1991 St. Helena Hwy., Rutherford, 707-968-1100;
800-782-4266; www.niebaum-coppola.com

Peju Province Winery
8466 St. Helena Hwy., Rutherford, 707-963-3600;
800-446-7358; www.peju.com

Prager Winery & Port Works
1281 Lewelling Ln., St. Helena, 707-963-7678; 800-969-7678;
www.pragerport.com

Robert Mondavi Winery
7801 St. Helena Hwy., Oakville, 707-963-9611; 888-766-6328;
www.robertmondavi.com

Rutherford Hill Winery
200 Rutherford Hill Rd., Rutherford, 707-963-1871;
800-637-5681; www.rutherfordhill.com

Sawyer Cellars
8350 St. Helena Hwy., Rutherford, 707-963-1980;
800-818-2252; www.sawyercellars.com

Schramsberg Vineyards
1400 Schramsberg Rd., Calistoga, 707-942-6668;
800-877-3623; www.schramsberg.com

Stag's Leap Wine Cellars
5766 Silverado Trail, Napa, 707-265-2441; 866-422-7523;
www.cask23.com

St. Clement Vineyards
2867 St. Helena Hwy. N., St. Helena, 707-967-3033;
800-331-8266; www.stclement.com

Sterling Vineyards
1111 Dunaweal Ln., Calistoga, 707-942-3344;
www.sterlingvineyards.com

St. Supery Vineyards & Winery
8440 St. Helena Hwy., Rutherford, 707-963-4507;
800-942-0809; www.stsupery.com

Sutter Home Winery
277 St. Helena Hwy. S., St. Helena, 707-963-3104;
www.sutterhome.com

Trefethen Vineyards
1160 Oak Knoll Ave., Napa, 707-255-7700; www.trefethen.com

V. Sattui Winery
1111 White Ln., St. Helena, 707-963-7774; 800-799-2337;
www.vsattui.com

Sonoma County

Alexander Valley Vineyards
8644 Hwy. 128, Healdsburg, 707-433-7209; 800-888-7209;
www.avvwine.com

Armida Winery
2201 Westside Rd., Healdsburg, 707-433-2222; www.armida.com

Arrowood Vineyards & Winery
14347 Sonoma Hwy., Glen Ellen, 707-935-2600;
800-938-5170; www.arrowoodwinery.com

Benziger Family Winery
1883 London Ranch Rd., Glen Ellen, 707-935-3000;
888-490-2739; www.benziger.com

B.R. Cohn Winery
15000 Sonoma Hwy., Glen Ellen, 707-938-4064;
800-330-4064; www.brcohn.com

Buena Vista Carneros
18000 Old Winery Rd., Sonoma, 707-938-1266;
www.buenavistawinery.com

California Welcome Center & Tasting Bar
9 Fourth St., Santa Rosa, 707-577-8674; 800-404-7673;
www.visitsantarosa.com

Cellar Door Tasting Room, The
The Lodge at Sonoma, 1395 Broadway, Ste. E, Sonoma,
707-938-4466

Chateau Souverain
400 Souverain Rd., Geyserville, 707-433-3141; 888-809-4637;
www.chateausouverain.com

Chateau St. Jean & Winery
8555 Sonoma Hwy. 12, Kenwood, 707-833-4134;
800-543-7572; www.chateaustjean.com

Cline Cellars
24737 Arnold Dr./Hwy. 121, Sonoma, 707-940-4000;
800-546-2070; www.clinecellars.com

Dry Creek Vineyard
3770 Lambert Bridge Rd., Healdsburg, 707-433-1000;
800-864-9463; www.drycreekvineyard.com

Family Wineries of Sonoma
9200 Sonoma Hwy. 12, Kenwood, 707-833-5504;
www.familywineries.com

Ferrari-Carano Vineyards & Winery
8761 Dry Creek Rd., Healdsburg, 707-433-6700;
800-831-0381; www.ferrari-carano.com

Field Stone Winery & Vineyard
10075 Hwy. 128, Healdsburg, 707-433-7266; 800-544-7273;
www.fieldstonewinery.com

Foppiano Vineyards
12707 Old Redwood Hwy., Healdsburg, 707-433-7272;
www.foppiano.com

Geyser Peak Winery
22281 Chianti Rd., Geyserville, 707-857-9400; 800-255-9463;
www.geyserpeakwinery.com

Gloria Ferrer Champagne Caves
23555 Hwy. 121, Sonoma, 707-996-7256; www.gloriaferrer.com

Gundlach-Bundschu Winery
2000 Denmark St., Sonoma, 707-938-5277; www.gunbun.com

Hop Kiln Winery
6050 Westside Rd., Healdsburg, 707-433-6491;
www.hopkilnwinery.com

Imagery Estate Winery
14335 Hwy. 12, Glen Ellen, 877-550-4278; 800-989-8890;
www.imagerywinery.com

Iron Horse Vineyards
9786 Ross Station Rd., Sebastopol, 707-887-1507;
www.ironhorsevineyards.com

J. Fritz Winery
24691 Dutcher Creek Rd., Cloverdale, 707-894-3389;
800-418-9643; www.fritzwinery.com

Jordan Vineyard & Winery
1474 Alexander Valley Rd., Healdsburg, 707-431-5250;
800-654-1213; www.jordanwinery.com

Kendall-Jackson Wine Center
5007 Fulton Rd., Fulton, 707-571-7500; www.kj.com

Kenwood Vineyards
9592 Sonoma Hwy. 12, Kenwood, 707-833-5891;
www.kenwoodvineyards.com

Korbel Champagne Cellars
13250 River Rd., Guerneville, 707-824-7000; 800-656-7235;
www.korbel.com

Kunde Estate Winery
10155 Sonoma Hwy. 12, Kenwood, 707-833-5501;
www.kunde.com

Landmark Vineyards
101 Adobe Canyon Rd., Kenwood, 707-833-0053;
800-452-6365; www.landmarkwine.com

Ledson Winery
7335 Hwy. 12, Santa Rosa, 707-537-3810;
www.ledson.com

Locals: A Collective Tasting Room
21023A Geyserville Ave., Geyserville, 707-857-4900;
www.tastelocalwines.com

Matanzas Creek Winery
6097 Bennett Valley Rd., Santa Rosa; 800-590-6464;
www.matanzascreek.com

Ravenswood Winery
18701 Gehricke Rd., Sonoma, 707-938-1960; 888-669-4679;
www.ravenswood-wine.com

Rodney Strong Vineyards
11455 Old Redwood Hwy., Healdsburg, 707-431-1533;
800-678-4763; www.rodneystrong.com

Rosenblum Cellars
250 Center St., Healdsburg, 707-431-1169;
www.rosenblumcellars.com

Sable Ridge Vineyards
6320 Jamison Rd., Santa Rosa, 707-542-3138;
www.sableridge.com

Sebastiani Vineyards
389 Fourth St. E., Sonoma, 707-933-3200; 800-888-5532;
www.sebastiani.com

Simi Winery
16275 Healdsburg Ave., Healdsburg, 707-433-6981;
800-746-4880; www.simiwinery.com

Sonoma-Cutrer Vineyards
4401 Slusser Rd., Windsor, 707-528-1181;
www.sonomacutrer.com

Trentadue Winery & Vineyards
19170 Geyserville Ave., Geyserville, 707-433-3104;
888-332-3032; www.trentadue.com

Viansa Winery & Italian Marketplace
25200 Hwy. 121, Sonoma, 707-935-4700; 800-995-4740;
www.viansa.com

Wine Room, The
9575 Sonoma Hwy., Kenwood, 707-833-6131;
www.the-wine-room.com

Mendocino County

Fetzer Tasting Room
45070 Main St., Mendocino, 707-937-6190; www.fetzer.com

Fetzer Vineyards
13601 Eastside Rd., Hopland, 707-744-1250;
www.fetzer.com

Frey Vineyards
14000 Tomki Rd., Redwood Valley, 707-485-5177;
800-760-3739; www.freywine.com

Greenwood Ridge Vineyards
5501 Hwy. 128, Philo, 707-895-2002;
www.greenwoodridge.com

Handley Cellars
3151 Hwy. 128, Philo, 707-895-3876; 800-733-3151;
www.handleycellars.com

Husch Vineyards
4400 Hwy. 128, Philo, 707-895-3216; 800-554-8724;
www.huschvineyards.com

Jepson Winery & Distillery
10400 S. Hwy. 101, Ukiah, 707-468-8936; 800-516-7342;
www.jepsonwine.com

McDowell Valley Vineyards
3811 Hwy. 175, Hopland, 707-744-1053;
www.mcdowellsyrah.com

Mendocino Specialty Vineyards
17810 Farrer Ln., Boonville, 707-895-3993

Navarro Vineyards
5601 Hwy. 128, Philo, 707-895-3686; 800-537-9463;
www.navarrowine.com

Pacific Echo
8501 Hwy. 128, Philo, 707-895-2957; 800-824-7754;
www.pacific-echo.com

Parducci Wine Cellars
501 Parducci Rd., Ukiah, 707-463-5350; 888-362-9463;
www.parducci.com

Redwood Valley Cellars Tasting Room
7051 N. State St., Redwood Valley, 707-485-0322;
www.redwoodvalleycellars.com

Roederer Estate
4501 Hwy. 128, Philo, 707-895-2288

For more information:

Napa Valley Vintners Association
P.O. Box 141, St. Helena, 707-963-3388;
www.napavintners.com

Sonoma Valley Vintners & Growers Alliance
17964 Sonoma Hwy., Sonoma, 707-935-0803;
www.sonomavalleywine.com

Mendocino Winegrowers Alliance
P.O. Box 1409, Ukiah, 707-468-9886; www.mendowine.com

Wine Vintage Chart

Prepared by our friend Howard Stravitz, this chart is designed to help you select wine to go with your meal.

	'85	'86	'88	'89	'90	'94	'95	'96	'97	'98	'99	'00	'01	'02
WHITES														
French:														
Alsace	24	18	22	28	28	26	25	24	24	26	24	26	27	–
Burgundy	26	25	–	24	22	–	29	28	24	23	25	24	21	–
Loire Valley	–	–	–	–	24	–	20	23	22	–	24	25	23	–
Champagne	28	25	24	26	29	–	26	27	24	24	25	25	26	–
Sauternes	21	28	29	25	27	–	21	23	26	24	24	24	28	–
California (Napa, Sonoma, Mendocino):														
Chardonnay	–	–	–	–	–	–	25	21	25	24	24	22	26	–
Sauvignon Blanc/Semillon	–	–	–	–	–	–	–	–	–	–	25	25	23	27	–
REDS														
French:														
Bordeaux	24	25	24	26	29	22	26	25	23	25	24	27	24	–
Burgundy	23	–	21	24	27	–	26	28	25	22	28	22	20	24
Rhône	25	19	27	29	29	24	25	23	24	28	27	26	25	–
Beaujolais	–	–	–	–	–	–	–	–	22	21	24	25	18	20
California (Napa, Sonoma, Mendocino):														
Cab./Merlot	26	26	–	21	28	29	27	25	28	23	26	23	26	–
Pinot Noir	–	–	–	–	–	26	23	23	25	24	26	25	27	–
Zinfandel	–	–	–	–	–	25	22	23	21	22	24	–	25	–
Italian:														
Tuscany	26	–	24	–	26	22	25	20	29	24	28	26	25	–
Piedmont	26	–	26	28	29	–	23	27	27	25	25	26	23	–